BE YOUR OWN GUIDE

WHERE SCIENCE & SPIRITUALITY MEET -THE
LAW OF ATTRACTION AND AFFIRMATION
HANDBOOK

RACHEL RIGGIO

ELEVATED
PUBLISHING

May all beings everywhere, and which we are inseparably connected, be fulfilled, awakened, liberated, and free. May there be peace in this world and throughout the entire universe. May we all together complete the spiritual journey.

BUDDHIST PRAYER

This book is dedicated to humanity.

It's dedicated to every person on the spiritual path of peace through self-awareness and connection. I dedicate this book to all my brothers and sisters in the world with gratitude for all the blessings that the universe has given us. May we collectively rise and collectively thrive as a community and family of humanity.

This book is also dedicated to:

The Red Road Foundation

The "red road" is a Native American spiritual term that describes being aware of how your life influences the world around you. It's the pathway to truth, peace, and harmony. I hope we can all rise in consciousness and walk the good red road together. We are a free education center working our way to self-sustainability. Rachel Riggio is a co-founder of this organization. As such, Rachel lives full-time in Kampot, Cambodia to support this initiative.

Website: https://theredroadfoundation.org

*Proceeds from this book and others benefit the foundation

TABLE OF CONTENTS

INTRODUCTION

Life is a crazy ride! We are all on it together and trying to make sense of it. Some of us live in abundance and others in scarcity. Who determines that? I believe we do. With all the suffering in the world, we may sometimes wonder what's the point? Where am I supposed to be getting to with all this? My answer is: right here, right now. They say life is a journey and I ask, "Are you enjoying it?" For me, that is how I define success. So, how do we learn to have peace with this wild world and these crazy times? I have been trying to figure out what's the point of it all since my days of childhood trauma. Life has been full of love, suffering, and surprises galore.

Through self-reflection, reading, practicing, meditating, failing, succeeding and all else, I have found a recipe that works for me. I have a beautiful life and I enjoy it every day. Even when things get really hard, I always know that it's all part of a process and it's all ok. It is a state of mind that is our divine mission to reach where we live in abundance. We are meant to thrive. Everything is vibration and frequency; we simply need to raise our vibration to have a different life. It may not sound plausible to some people, but the idea is scientifically supported. Even the scientists at NASA have confirmed that human cells respond physically to frequencies.

In most societies today, we have been programmed to be fearful and feel unworthy. The news always keeps us worrying and the commercials keep us feeling inadequate. It lowers the frequency of our bodies and keeps us from our true potential. We are enough. We have the ability to thrive and live in harmony. We are love! We are eternal beings that come back to learn our life lessons and learn how to use these incredible tools we call the human body and mind. There are magnificent and magical things all around us every day, but we have to train the mind to start seeing those things and being in a state of gratitude for them.

Everything is a frequency and a vibration. It is proven by the science of cymatics. It is the organizational foundation for the creation of all matter in life. These waves have a direct impact on the structures that they move through, like our cells. The resonance of our being is our responsibility. What are we tuning in to? We are an interpretation of our environment. Getting disciplined about what we think and surround ourselves with will change our experience of life.

Affirmations can keep us rooted on the journey when life takes over and we forget. We are taking authority over our mind's chatter and remembering why we are here. We are reprogramming our minds for success and to attract abundance. When we can ground ourselves in how amazing the natural world is, we can remember that we are perfectly a part of it. Tesla said, "If you want to find the secrets of the universe, think in terms of energy, frequency, and vibration."

My intention for this book is to share the information that has transformed every facet of my life. I believe we are one and I am part of a movement that is happening across the universe where we collectively rise to thrive. Put your conditioned beliefs to the side and just try to open your mind to these perspectives. If they don't align with your belief system, that's ok. You can easily return to your present state. But maybe, just maybe this book will transform your life and influence all the life that you come into contact with.

Watch your thoughts, they become your words; watch your words, they become your actions; watch your actions, they become your habits; watch your habits, they become your character; watch your character, it becomes your destiny.

LAO TZU

THE ORIGIN

ffirmations are positive sentences we repeat to ourselves in order to break our maladaptive neural-nets, also known as neural networks or neural circuits. Neural-nets are the unconscious loops in our brain where nerves have formed long-term relationships in which stimuli is interpreted into emotion. In other words, you see something that reminds you of something else, which makes you feel a certain way. Your brain is trained to feel certain ways when you see things that trigger memories.

Thoughts will produce chemical reactions in the brain that affect our bodies. We all have nerve networks in our brains that lead us to various emotional experiences that we call our "state of being." These are based on unique and personal stimuli that stem from how we have been conditioned. What may lead one person to a state of despair could lead another to complete trust in the universe. It is all a matter of association and perspective.

These nerve cells are "wired" together from repetition. For example, if I woke up every morning to absolute chaos in my house, I would associate mornings and waking up with chaos. If I want to change my experience and have good mornings, I will need to re-associate waking up with a new emotional state. At this point, my brain automatically feels chaotic and stressed at 8:00 every morning. Even if I now live in a place where it is peaceful in the morning, I may still associate mornings with chaos. My brain automatically expects chaos when I open my eyes, so I wake up in an emotional state that is undesirable. Therefore, I will need to break this neural network and rewire my brain to associate mornings with calmness, opportunity and gratitude.

These neural networks are formed by repetitive patterns over time and associating the same stimuli with specific emotional responses. Affirmations have been proven to interrupt these associations to reprogram the mind. They were created by two neuroscientists in the 1970s with neuro-linguistic backgrounds. They believed that increasing positive words and behaviors would lead to more personal success and lasting happiness. Affirmations were invented for use in modern society with the intention of disturbing these neural circuits in our brains that bring us dissatisfying life perceptions. Their research showed that we could rewire our brains through replacing self-defeating neural pathways with positive beliefs that lead to uplifting emotional states. The term "neuroplasticity" is used to describe the capability of our brains to be molded and reorganized to produce different chemical reactions. They found that we can make new neural-networks by being disciplined in interrupting our faulty reaction patterns. This model is replacing destructive, self-limiting thoughts with positive associations that lead to uplifting emotions and confidence. How we think determines how we feel, and how we feel directly affects what we think. So, affirmations can help us reach more positive emotions in our bodies so that we can start to make shifts in our state of being.

Affirmations are similar to mantras and have similar long-term effects. Mantras are ancient sayings chanted during meditation that help to keep the mind from wandering down non-productive avenues. Their Sanskrit roots translate to liberating one's thinking. The purpose of mantras is to help free the mind of incessant human brain chatter. They are meant to reprogram and train our minds. When your thoughts keep getting sucked up into a wheel of self-limiting judgements, your chanting will root you to great truths and the inner workings of the universe. The truth is, we simply cannot believe and identify with everything that we think! There is so much information that our brains are taking in subconsciously, and many times societal pressures make fearful thinking the norm. But with affirmations or mantras, we are choosing to silence the chatter that robs us of our energy and instead place our focus on something that reinforces our true potential and goals. Regularly practiced with sincerity, both of these tools have been proven to improve relationships, decrease stress, lead to more personal success, and reinforce confidence and emotional well-being.

THE PHILOSOPHY

You are the universe experiencing itself.

ALAN WATTS

Who are we really? What forms our concept of who we are? How do we know for certain "Who am I?" I was listening to Wayne Dyer speak about his book called *Wishes Fulfilled*. He said that the words "I am" are the most powerful two words in the world. This really got me thinking. Could this be true? He says that what you declare you are is what you are indeed. We are what we think, say and do. If I say "I am sad" every day, my concept of who I am is sad. What I think is sad, what I feel is sad, how I act is sad and what I invite into my life is sad. We attract what we are. We are what we say we are and what we practice. I purposely try not to say, "I am sad." If I feel sad, I say, "I feel sad." "Am" is a state of being, and feelings are temporary. If I declare that "I am an eternal being," then suffering doesn't feel so overwhelming; it feels temporary.

Let's say that on the way to work in traffic every morning, I tell myself that "I am so tired of this." I will be so tired of driving in traffic every morning. I will dread the ride, and I will keep my body in a state of frustration and stress. So, I release cortisol (the stress hormone) in my body, and it affects the rest of my day and my health. Let's say I want to reprogram my mind, and I see that morning drive as an opportunity. I start a new routine of listening to podcasts on the law of attraction and practicing my affirmations every morning on the way to work. This way, I can change how I feel in the morning. It will be a self-awareness challenge that I invite into my life. Practicing this will change my energy levels for the day. I am changing my behavior, which leads to different thoughts and different emotional states. I can start practicing my affirmation when I get into the car: "I am so grateful to have this quiet time for spiritual knowledge." Through doing this, who and what you are on the way to work will change. If you change this routine and self-talk, it will be the beginning of a new and very empowering relationship with yourself. Your relationship with yourself can literally transform you and what opportunities you attract into your life.

Anytime you start a sentence with 'I AM,' you are creating what you are and what you want to be.

DR. WAYNE DYER

I've been on quite a spiritual journey over the past few years. I have striven to become completely aware of everything I think and say. Yes, this sounds like something we should always be doing, naturally. In reality, there's so much that goes through our minds and out through our mouths that doesn't truly align with what we believe and who we really are. It was an experiment for me to see if the way that I felt would change if I became completely aware of what I told myself or declared about myself. In truth, my whole life has changed, and approaching each moment, each word, each thought, as sacred and meaningful is one of the most simple and profound experiences I've ever had. I became aware that most of us have been programmed to be miserable. Most "I am" thoughts center around unworthiness that is reinforced by superficial ads for a perfect life. We are taught that material goods will make us happy, but in my experience, it is the most materialistic people who seem the most unhappy. Without realizing it, we buy into the priorities that don't bring true contentment and peace.

So, who am I? I am love. I am an eternal being. I hold the vision for my ideal future, and I trust the process of my life. I am co-creating a life of abundance with the divine. I am a magnet for love and money. I share my gifts and talents to raise the vibration of the world around me. My needs are always met. I am grateful. I am One with the natural world.

3

THE SCIENCE

Everything is energy, and that's all there is to it. Match the frequency of the energy you want, and you cannot help but get that reality. It can be no other way. This is not philosophy. This is physics.

ALBERT EINSTEIN

We have all heard that like attracts like. That is science, and it is the foundation of the law of attraction. The law of attraction is a belief system that we attract what we are. It has been scientifically proven that two things vibrating at the same frequency will be pulled together. So, when we spend our time worrying, we attract more to worry about. When we spend our time in gratitude, we attract more to be grateful for. I am a huge fan of Dr. Joe Dispenza. He is a well-known neuroscientist who has literally transformed the lives of thousands of people around the world. He had a traumatic injury and was told by doctors that he needed a very risky and painful surgery that would leave him in a body cast for a year. He decided to decline the surgery and heal himself with his mind. He did so and now travels the world helping people to learn their true power and have spontaneous remissions. In his seminars, people have made miraculous recoveries. Blind people have started to see, people with irreversible diseases have spontaneously healed and people have learned how to attract the things they desire into their lives. Everything he does is backed by scientific proof and statistics. On a deeper level, this means we all have a piece of the creator within us, and through learning how to utilize our powers of manifestation, we can create the life of our dreams here on Earth. A couple of years ago, I may have thought that this all sounded a bit crazy and far-fetched. However, when practicing mindfulness with all my thoughts and words, I have watched the things that I have told myself come true.

There's a documentary called "What the Bleep Do We Know." It's about quantum physics. The documentary mentions a study by a man named Dr. Masaru Emoto. He does studies with water molecules and intention. In his experiment, he took photographs of magnified water molecules. He infused different samples of water with either negative or positive intentions. He photographed them both before and after infusing them with the intention. His findings were incredible! The water molecules into which he had put love, peace and gratitude formed into beautiful crystals that looked like snowflakes. The water that he had infused with hateful messages looked mutated, distorted and were not in organized patterns. He then made the point that our bodies are made up of over 50% water and asked us to contemplate what our thoughts can do to our own bodies.

I have first-hand experience with seeing the negative manifestations of people who are constantly worrying and affirming the scarcity in their lives. I have seen these thoughts create disease and illness in their/our bodies. I also had the experience of curing myself of cystic acne and sciatica by becoming aware of my thoughts with dedication and compassion. I interrupted my negative thoughts and replaced them with deep breaths followed by my heartfelt affirmation. I don't want to put fear and stress into my body. Anytime I feel frustrated, worried or anxious, I return to my practice.

4

THE REALITY

How you think, how you act and how you feel is called your personality, and your personality creates your personal reality. When you change your personality, you change your personal reality.

DR. JOE DISPENZA

Now, I'm completely aware that there is lots of new-age terminology and concepts that can seem a bit "out there." There are some claims that may turn people off, and then there's the true "magic" of life and manifestation. These are ancient secrets and divine wisdom that lives in all life. We just have not been taught how to harness this power. Once I began learning about these things and practicing them every day, I've been completely blown away and astonished to see my manifestations show up in my life so perfectly and unexpectedly. I have a disciplined practice that I will explain. It is tied to my "I am" affirmations. The things I've learned and embodied over the past couple of years have been so profoundly powerful that I feel I must share them. I want to shout it from the rooftops so that we may all rise together. I believe that if we were all taught this, our families, communities and world could truly thrive. But it all starts with one person who raises the level of consciousness for all he or she comes into contact with.

Just like everyone, I've been through immense challenges and struggles in my life: depression, trauma, abuse, suicidal thoughts, anxiety, grief, jealousy, anger, unworthiness and self-sabotaging patterns. I think at this uncertain time in the world, most of us have struggled with these things. Though we are all struggling with very similar things, our social media profiles project a beautiful, perfect world. This just leaves us unfulfilled and feeling like we are missing out. Usually, we see those images and it makes us think about what we don't have, making us feel down, unworthy and less than. We think "I am never going to have that" or "I am not lucky like them." Now, there is another perspective to see those images from. Through the power of visualization, I can imagine the life I want to manifest and feel how it would be to experience that. People talk about the "work" you do on yourself to attract positive things into your life with the law of attraction. Well, here it is: Get yourself to feel grateful for what you want before you have it. It is not easy, but it can be done. This is why visualization is such a powerful tool. It will help you to imagine your dream life and feel how it would feel. Your brain releases the same chemicals when you experience something, visualize experiencing something, or see someone in a movie. When I send out gratitude for my dream life, I will attract back gratitude for my dream life. When I accept this as my future reality, I subconsciously take the steps to get me there. It is not a matter of if but when I get there.

Now, if I see someone in turquoise water with a custom bamboo bungalow in the jungle with the funds and freedom to travel the world with their soulmate, I am not jealous. No! Instead, I smile and use that as a source of inspiration. I imagine myself on that beach, with my lover and our custom-built home. I imagine what it would feel like to have that in my life until I believe that I will have that. I am moving toward that every day. I deserve that, and that reality exists in my future. This is called leveling up and changing your vibration, which in turn changes what you attract into your life.

5

THE WHY

Why get invested in affirmations? Affirmations are used to intercept our unconscious neural circuits, which directly affect how we feel. How we feel will then affect our behavior, and our behavior will then change our patterns. When we change our patterns, we make new habits. When we make new habits, we align with new frequencies (ways of being), and those frequencies will directly attract like frequencies into our environment.

Our environment is defined by the Merriam-Webster dictionary as the circumstances, objects or conditions by which one is surrounded. Now, we are all living in this world, and some of us live in heaven while others live in hell. Some people seem to always be the victim, always complaining and always being presented with more difficulty. Then, there are other people who seem to always be grateful and optimistic. We might wonder how they always have the luckiest circumstances. How do they attract the right people, just at the right time to carry out the things that they are manifesting in their lives? Well, there's actually science behind this.

Neuroplasticity refers to the reorganization of neural synapses in our brains that form new pathways from our conditioned responses/chemical reactions. These pathways grow and evolve with life experiences the triggers that we acquire. Each individual associates certain things with positive or negative feelings. There are circuits in the brain that lead to how we feel, and therefore how we behave. Some people start to feel sad when the sun goes down. Some people feel lucky when they see blue flowers. Others see the same flowers and remember a morning of abandonment. Some people see something that they want but don't have, so they start replaying a narrative of unworthiness for themselves.

This is where affirmations can really help. The number one most important step on the path to rewire your mind, as Dr. Joe Dispenza states, is to become aware of what you tell yourself. Can you become an observer of your own inner world? Through noticing how your brain goes from stimuli to feeling, you can choose to reinforce that association or replace it with an affirmation that takes you through a different neurological pathway that leads to a positive experience. Emotions are sending vibrations out to an energetic field that we call the universe. The law of attraction shows that what you are projecting is what you are receiving. The trick is figuring out how to feel gratitude for that which you desire before you have received it.

With neuroplasticity in mind, you become aware of rewiring the circuits in your brain. Where one image used to lead to a thought that leads to a self-defeating narrative, it can now have light shone on it, and one can consciously make the choice that leads to a new pathway in the brain. It is uncomfortable at first, but the more we practice it, the more it feels natural and right. So, if I usually start to feel down at sunset, then I start telling myself I'm lonely. This sends me into a series of overwhelming thoughts about how I will never find the love of my life. Once I become compassionately aware of that pattern, I am then able to begin using my affirmations to change it.

I compassionately and lovingly take three deep breaths, and then I say, "I am love, and I attract love. I am grateful for the day and night. I am grateful to attract deep connections into my life." I then imagine being love, projecting love and receiving love. I reaffirm to myself that I will have unconditional love, and I deserve that. I'll bring myself into the present moment of being love. I will breathe the feeling of love into every cell of my body and feel grateful. Now, if I do my breathing and affirmation every day at sunset when I feel myself starting to get sad, this is when I start to rewire the neural pathways in my brain. After about two weeks, it starts becoming much easier, and now, when the sun goes down, maybe instead of feeling lonely, I start to think about love and the visualizations that I am manifesting. I start to re-associate the sun going down with other feelings, other behaviors and therefore other habits. Now, we are remapping the mind.

Plasticity is defined as the capacity to be shaped and molded. So now, we are not victims of the patterns that have been programmed into us by our parents or our society. We are consciously rewiring our minds to bring us uplifting states of being. When we function from a higher consciousness and grateful vibration, our outer environment changes. This is why we do the work. We go through the uncomfort-able feelings and self-awareness mixed with self-discipline. Through doing this, we watch ourselves co-create the life of our dreams. We feel amazed, proud and humbled by the glory of this world we live in.

6

THE REWARDS

When I let go of what I am, I become what I might be.

LAO TZU

I want to live the abundant life of my dreams, be full of peace and gratitude. So, how can we employ this law of attraction that everyone's talking about? First, we must really understand it — not just conceptually, but really understand in the core of our beings that we attract what we are. What we are is what we think, say and do. The law of attraction mentality elevates our thinking to the big picture. Basically, it enforces that we are vibration. Everything can be seen as vibration instead of matter. Things are not set in stone but continuously evolving. The famous Alan Watts said that when he realized how much of what we call "matter" is actually waves and vibration, he was scared he might fall through the floor. Now, this was a joke, but he is right — most of what we are is vibration. Like attracts like. **We don't attract what we want; we attract what we are.**

This is something that we have to really understand on a deep level. Some people think that they can change matters by just repeating some positive affirmations a couple of times per day. But that's really not how it works. The law of attraction is about truly being and feeling what you want in your life. If I want to be rich, I need to feel what it would be like to have money flowing to me easily and picture and feel what I would be doing with it.

To have the love of my life show up, I need to visualize what it feels like to be held in my love's arms. I will feel the love flowing to and from me freely. I will have to align my vibration with that which I am inviting into my life. Affirmations are sentences that bring you to remember these states of mind and practice your ability to feel that way. It takes self-awareness and discipline to bring your mind to these places, especially when you have been feeling fear or scarcity. Through repetition and sincere dedication, harnessing the law of attraction will become easier.

By using affirmations as a tool, we can intercept the neural pathways in our minds that have been keeping us stuck and unhappy. Once we become aware of what those maps (neural networks) are, we can start to interrupt them with the practice of breath and affirmation. New brain circuits will bring new opportunities into our lives. So, I use the affirmation to level up and start feeling myself from a place of gratitude that already has all of the things I desire. I use my gratitude for everything I already have to gain emotional momentum.

I think about all the functions of my body, how I can move my finger just by thinking it, the wind on my skin, the moon pulling the waves, the feathers of a bird, the roots of trees and all the privileges of being alive with my five senses. Meditating on all the things we have to be grateful for will actually grow the electromagnetic field around the heart, which has been scientifically proven and measured through the work of Dr. Dispenza. When I grow the energetic field around my heart, I am attracting things to be grateful for.

When we take the time to practice affirmations and meditation, we can get to truly know our minds. So often, we run away from uncomfortable feelings, trying to numb ourselves or pour ourselves into work, sex or food to avoid just being honest and accepting the truth. But, if we stand there and face those uncomfortable feelings, we move through them and notice what it is that we are saying to ourselves right before we start to run away. If we can fearlessly get to know ourselves, have compassion for ourselves, notice what is programmed in our minds and have a disciplined routine to intercept our program, we can truly reach new levels of consciousness. Through this new awareness, we will have more peace and trust that we will attract what is meant for us.

We are all on a spiritual journey to learn how to use our innate powers of co-creation to manifest the abundant life of our dreams. One of the beautiful things about life is that you never have to go out searching for your lesson. Your lesson will always appear in physical form right before your eyes. We manifest exactly what we need to work through.

Many times, it comes in the form of our relationships with those who hold up mirrors to us. We can fight the other person and try to make them wrong, or we can look in that mirror and learn to fearlessly have compassion and love for that person.

How we treat others and our environment is how we treat ourselves. It is a mission in my life to mindfully approach all moments in life as sacred opportunities. This happens when we cultivate a good relationship with our higher selves and can connect with spiritual laws and trust over fear and resistance. When we can visualize and believe in the ultimate vision for our lives, we subconsciously take the steps necessary to achieve it. Not only that, but when the intention is clear, the powers of creation can aid you by sending people, circumstances and opportunity directly to you. It sounds like magic (I think universal laws are quite magical), but it is backed by science. So, how do we do it?

7

THE HOW

If you correct your mind, the rest of your life will fall into place.

LAO TZU

Meditation is a practice of getting to know yourself. When you sit down to meditate, you start breathing in and out and put all your energy into simply breathing and being. Now, most people are going to start having random thoughts come up in your mind. Many times, it's the inner critic that comes out telling you that you don't have time to sit around and close your eyes doing nothing, or maybe you start thinking about something causing stress in your life, or maybe just a weird commercial that you saw last week. Anyway, this is what they call the "monkey mind." Wikipedia describes it as "a Buddhist term meaning an "unsettled; restless; capricious; whimsical; fanciful; inconstant; confused; indecisive; uncontrollable" mind.

What we want to do is become familiar with the monkey mind. Notice when the chatter starts; be aware of it. Take inventory of the thoughts and the physical discomforts that you have during that moment. Half the battle is stopping and noticing what you feel like when stress starts coming over your body because of things that you're telling yourself. When you can hear that voice and decide not to identify with what it is telling you, you will have reached a new state of being. You will be in control of the only thing you can truly control in this life—your mind. Most people are slaves to this part of the mind and the urges of the five senses. Most people just let it keep them in dissatisfaction, moving from one thing to another without truly being present.

You can hear the monkey mind start and choose to not identify with it. You can choose to connect with your higher self instead. You can choose to see the big picture in any situation. Personally, I will start feeling the heaviness over my shoulders and pressure behind my neck, and I begin to clench my jaw a bit. Noticing with compassion is the first important step to making friends with yourself. Just notice that it's happening.

Some people like to name the inner critic voice, and some can begin to recognize it when you feel the physical sensations coming over your body. When this happens, we simply and lovingly take a big deep breath in, filling up with all of the amazing life force in this world. Personally, I think about the force of the wind, the expansiveness of the stars, creatures of the deep sea, intricate flowers, vastness of mountains and canyons… all of the beautiful nature in this world. I picture myself filling up with that life force. I feel grateful to know that I am one with it all. Afterwards, I take a deep breath out, pushing from my belly and picturing all of the incessant chatter of the human mind as black smoke, which I blow out. I do it three times and then I repeat my affirmation or mantra. "I am eternal, my suffering is temporary. I trust the process. I attract abundance. I am love. My needs are always met. I am meant to thrive," are my go-to affirmations.

This will be the disciplined habit for grounding. Every time you're in meditation or out of meditation, when you feel the sensation of the monkey mind, take three deep breaths to re-center and ground yourself in the present moment. During this PRACTICE, you fill yourself up with the life force strength and ground yourself back down into your true belief system with your affirmation. To break a habit, we have to recondition ourselves and rewire the pathways in our brain that lead us to transcending our self-sabotaging loops.

Difficult emotions come with unexpected events and are necessary for growing and becoming better people. But negative self-talk is something that does not benefit our forward movement. We are learning to fearlessly endure life's hardships and be able to go through things like grief, embarrassment, failure or anxiety and come out the other side with an overall trust in the process. One of my favorite quotes is, "Hold the vision; trust the process." This is big-picture thinking that works very well for affirmations because it takes you out of the monkey mind loop and puts things in perspective.

If you have enjoyed this book so far, then please take a moment and leave a review. Not only do we appreciate hearing feedback from our readers, but the more reviews this book receives, the more visible it becomes to other readers. Perhaps this book has made an impact on your life and you would like to share that experience with others—the best way in doing so is not only through a positive review, but also word of mouth. Thank you in advance for any feedback you leave! Also, please consider visiting Rachel Riggio's Website. Now, we shall resume with the following chapter.

8

AFFIRMATION CREATION

How can we pick the right affirmations for us? An affirmation needs to reinforce a vision of what we are calling into our lives and reinforce the positive qualities that we have. Remember, what we give our attention to will grow. If I continually affirm that I am love, I will make more loving decisions and attract more love back to me. We attract what we ARE. One of the most important things about affirmations is to feel the words when you say them. When I tell myself, "I am love," I open my heart and really connect to being love. We must pick something that really takes us to a strong feeling in our bodies.

Emotion is energy in motion.

PETER MCWILLIAMS

It is what you are sending out into a field of vibrations that will come back to you. What you put your attention into is what grows. In this case, your emotion is like the radio tower that is sending out the vibrations or frequencies that you want to receive back. The law of attraction says that like attracts like. So, the affirmation that you embody for these breaths should have a deep emotion tied to it. For me, I like to use something quite broad that reminds me who I am and where I am going. I like to repeat, "I am love. I trust the process. What is meant for me will come to me."

If you want to find the secrets of the universe, think in terms of energy, frequency and vibration.

NIKOLA TESLA

Many people learn about affirmations when trying to create success in their lives, achieve weight loss, transcend low self-esteem or self-worth, build confidence, cure insomnia, or heal from divorce. The pain they are in drives them to cultivate new habits that could potentially bring peace and abundance. It is our pain that shows us where we need to grow.

When picking your affirmations, it is important to really understand what your monkey mind is telling you and where you really are getting hooked by your pain and fear. We must dissect the thoughts that we have tied to the limiting beliefs that put us down and rob us of our energy. These thoughts are things that we most likely do not even truly believe but that we were potentially told enough times that we adopted them as truth. We must break it down for ourselves and notice these thoughts and the feelings they cause. These are often tied to childhood traumas or long exposure to toxic relationships. They are rooted in fear, and our goal is to use them to know when to compassionately hug that inner child within. We need to affirm to them that everything is okay. Sometimes it can look like we are reparenting ourselves. We often don't realize that we tell ourselves things that we were told as children. Many times our needs were not met, and we learned that the world is an unsafe place where needs don't get met. This is the basis of what we need to overcome. We need to create a safe place in ourselves where we can self-soothe and know that difficult times will always come to an end.

When I took the time and discipline to really understand what was causing me suffering in my own mind, I learned the root. For me, the root was that I'm not doing enough. I always put pressure on myself to do more, and I felt guilty about just being and taking things in. Every time I wanted to relax, I would start to clench my jaw and think about all the things I had to do. I would put pressure on myself that would not allow me to enjoy the present moment. I would say things to myself like, "You don't have time. You're wasting time. You could be doing more." I was raised by a single mom who always told us that she didn't have time to relax, and I think I adopted this mentality. I also always felt too much responsibility for the suffering of others and took it upon myself to try to make it all better. I tried to take away the pain of my mom after my dad died, and I think it became tied to my concept of my role in the world. It would put me in a low and defeated vibration where I didn't feel inspired to work or enjoy. It was too much pressure with no enjoyment of the fruits of my labor or appreciation of the moment. It cut off my creative inspiration and took me out of the "flow."

When we are not rooted in the present moment, the energy of the creation cannot flow through us. People call this many different things — Chi, Wu Wei or the divine energy. It is when you're in "flow state" that you have no resistance to life on life's terms. You do what you love, and it moves through you effortlessly. It's when people, situations and circumstances naturally line up for you to be able to accomplish your goals with ease. But we must be grounded and rooted in the present moment to be able to assess the flow. Affirmations can be used to keep us here. I used my affirmations to pull myself out of that anxiety and stress that was holding me back from experiencing the state of flow. I noticed the physical sensation and negative thoughts, so I took my three breaths and affirmed. Then I was back in my body and in the moment.

There was an article on Healthline that gave some very clear instructions for creating your own affirmations. The first was to begin with "I" or "my." What we want to do is to truly identify with the affirmation. The second is to keep our affirmations in the present tense. This way you know that right now in this present moment, you have what it takes. It is not something that may or may not happen in the future. Next, we want to make sure that we keep our affirmations positive. We don't want to use words like "won't," "don't" or "not." For example, "I won't identify with negative thought patterns" should be changed to "I am bigger than my thoughts" or "I am an eternal being who is greater than the monkey mind." Another example is, "I don't want unhealthy love" to "I am love. I attract healthy, unconditional love into my life." The next step in creating a good affirmation is to link them to something that is in alignment with your core value system. Take time to sit down with yourself and think about the big picture of life and what you truly believe. Can you compassionately observe yourself, look at your patterns, and see how your behaviors and thoughts have warranted specific outcomes (especially if they are recurring).

The oldest symbol for humanity is the great spiral. It shows how we have a set of patterns and life lessons running through our lives. We go through the highs and lows like waves. Then we become aware of ourselves and the pattern itself. The pattern usually stems from things that we normalized in childhood but are unhealthy ways to think and behave. Once we see our pattern, we are conscious of how we move from the highs and the lows. Each time we hit that bottom of the spiral, we know we will go through another loop and another loop until we can be completely at peace with the ways of the world. We come to peace and contentment in the middle of the spiral, accepting life on life's terms and enjoying the journey. Writing or sharing your life story with a friend could help. We normalize our day-to-day emotions, and sometimes it's hard to even notice what is or is not part of our faulty belief system. Through truly knowing yourself and having compassion for yourself, you will live your life in a different way. I highly recommend printing a picture of yourself as a child around 4 years old. Be sure that the way you speak to yourself today would care for and protect that inner child. It will help you as you are creating your affirmations based on what is meaningful to you and is truly at the root of what you are learning in this lifetime.

In the book, The Untethered Soul, Michael Singer explains the discussion between two parts of our mind. There's the human brain that can be a complete slave to the five senses and instant gratification. Then, there is the eternal part of our mind that some would call "the soul." Singer asks us to notice these discussions between these two parts of ourselves. Even though we can hear what the human mind has to say, we can put our faith in the eternal part of our consciousness. The soul knows that this incarnation is a learning experience, that we are okay, and that we have the ability to learn, live and grow to create the lives of our dreams. Of course, there will be suffering along the way, but the more we can just accept hard times and move through them, the closer we will get to having peace and living in a state of flow. We waste our energy resisting suffering, numbing ourselves and trying to not feel pain. This prolongs it, which manifests in toxic ways. When we can just surrender to life, let ourselves hurt when we need to and fearlessly walk through the pain, it will pass, and our lesson will become clear. When we live this way, there is nothing to fear. We are eternal, and we can expand our concept of this lifetime and of who we truly are.

> There is nothing more important to true growth than realizing that you are not the voice of the mind — you are the one who hears it.
>
> MICHAEL SINGER

When we come from a place of trust, gratitude and acceptance, hard times are just hard times; they aren't our identity. This was an amazing realization that was solidified for me after reading <u>Many Lives, Many Masters</u> by Brian Weiss, the psychiatrist, hypnotherapist and author who specializes in past life regression therapy. He is a graduate of Columbia and Yale School of Medicine who had firsthand experiences that transformed his views on life. He has a science background and had such an incredible spiritual experience with hypnosis that he transformed his whole life because of it. Another book that helped in this regard was <u>Proof of Heaven,</u> written by a neurosurgeon explaining his near-death experience and the way it changed his life. These books really put things into perspective by helping us see our hard times as opportunities to level up.

They were written by people who were not spiritual people; they built their lives on scientific principles. They both risked their reputations by writing these books because others in the field may have looked at them as different after sharing their transcendental experiences. It reminds us that all suffering is temporary, and the point of life is to grow beyond our conditioning to find peace and abundance. How can we work together to collectively thrive? This will bring us great joy. Understanding this helps us to connect to the big-picture thinking that affirmations reinforce.

9

THE DEVELOPMENT

Setting up the right affirmation will begin to change your brain little by little. As the neuroscience adage goes, the neurons that fire together, wire together. You will make these neurons begin to fire together by creating affirmations that build mental associations. Take the time to control your brain toward what you want, rather than leaving it to chance.

LERONE GRAHAM

During this period of deep introspection, you have sat alone, written and spoken about your story. Now, you have a compassionate understanding of what you learned in your early years and how you have recreated patterns in your adult life. What are the consistent lessons that you feel are repeating themselves in your life? For me, it's having faith that I will be taken care of. As I work toward making the world around me better, the universe will take care of me and bring me what I need. I often have worried that my needs would not be met. I lived in a fear of scarcity with sciatica keeping me in limited functionality. I constantly felt that I wasn't doing enough. I had trouble relaxing, and I was worried that my needs wouldn't be met. I clung to things for fear of losing what I loved. Through these behaviors and thoughts, I pushed away and blocked many loving and abundant experiences. So, knowing this is my pattern, I will now pick an affirmation that directly takes me out of the fear of scarcity. What is the opposite of fear of scarcity? It is the trust in the universe to provide and the inner knowledge that I deserve and can attract all the abundance available in the world. So, my affirmation will go to the root of this issue. I will affirm to myself, "My needs will be met. I deserve abundance. I am love. I trust in the universe. I am meant to thrive. What is meant for me is on its way to me." When I say these words to myself, I breathe deeply and know at the deepest level of my being that these words are true.

Once you have understood your pain point, you can develop what your affirmations are going to be. We have to stop identifying with the thoughts that are keeping us from experiencing joy and gratitude. It is possible to have peace with the ways of the world, even when things are hard. It is part of the great journey of life. Negative emotions show us where we need to grow and expand our vision of who we are. Affirmations can align us with a higher vantage point from which to view our lives. Realigning with the big picture and connecting to a greater vision for your life will help you to reprioritize as you rewire your mind. The following chapter contains examples of opportunities and affirmations directed towards those opportunities.

We're addicted to our beliefs; we're addicted to the emotions of our past. We see our beliefs as truths, not ideas that we can change... We've in fact conditioned ourselves to believe all sorts of things that aren't necessarily true — and many of these things are having a negative impact on our health and happiness.

DR. JOE DISPENZA

10

EXAMPLE PAIN POINTS & AFFIRMATIONS

The following pages contain examples of common ways that someone may be feeling, and affirmations that may help you transcend these feelings. We're calling these feelings "pain points," as each of the examples are a negative experience. We can rise from this negative self-talk with the redirection provided by the affirmations. As these are merely examples, you may take the following pain points and affirmations and reapply them to any other negative mindset by building your own similar affirmations. Perhaps use this chapter as an exercise and create additional affirmations that speak to you personally. Explore other pain points that are not mentioned and engage in this practice to change your psychology to that of a positive experience.

As soon as we free ourselves from the mirage of hurrying time, we are alive again, as in childhood, to the ecstasies of ordinary life.

ALAN WATTS

Feeling Unworthy

I am love. I radiate my love for the good of all.

I am whole, and I don't need to chase
anything to be complete.

I deserve love and abundance.

There is infinite wisdom within me. I am one
with the universe.

I am perfectly me. I love myself on the
journey to inner peace.

I positively impact the world around me.

Discontentment and Anxiety

I am right where I need to be. I hold the
vision for my life and trust the process.

Every day, I get closer to my goals. I am doing
enough.

I create a life of peace and success, step by
step.

Inner peace keeps me in a state of receiving
abundance.

I choose uplifting and powerful thoughts that
energize me and validate my efforts.

I am grateful.

Financial Issues

I create a life of abundance as I move towards my goals.

Every day I get closer to receiving the financial rewards of the energy I put into the world.

Money is an exchange of energy.

Money flows to me easily.

I generate abundance. I am grateful for my blessings.

Weight Loss

I am exactly where I am meant to be in the
process of becoming my potential.

I am whole. I fill myself up with the power of
love.

I am beautiful. I am grateful for my body.

My body is the greatest tool that I will ever
have.

I am my own unique interpretation of this
world. I am exactly where I am meant
to be.

I am present and grateful.

Divorce/Breakup

I am whole. I attract the lessons my soul
needs to learn.

I know my worth. I trust the process for my
life. I release control, and I trust the
process.

Whoever and whatever is meant for me will
flow to me. Love lifts me up and connects
me to all life.

I am love, and I attract love.

I am complete and satisfied on my own.

Loving relationships come to me effortlessly
when I am at peace with who I am.

I treat myself the way I deserve to be treated
by others, with unconditional love and
compassion.

Creating Success

I am powerful and creating the life of my dreams every day.

As I visualize my dream life, I take the conscious and subconscious steps towards making them my reality.

I attract abundance. I deserve the life of my dreams.

I set my intentions and I am clear on what I want.

I am a powerful being, capable of living in absolute abundance.

The perfect situations, people and circumstances flow into my life at the perfect times.

My needs are always met. I am present and grateful.

Depression

I am inseparable with the divine. I believe in
my ability to create the life of my dreams.

As I choose my thoughts, I align with what I
attract into my life.

I have the ability to make the world a better
place. My thoughts and actions are my
choice.

As I spread love and kindness, it flows back to
me effortlessly.

I change my thoughts and actions, and I build
myself a better, more fulfilled life.

I choose to identify with the thoughts that are
in alignment with my potential for
abundance in all aspects of my life.

I trust the process. I positively impact the
world around me.

Grief

I am an eternal being. I am love and vibration.
My soul lives forever.

I connect with my soulmates throughout
lifetimes. I trust in a higher plan for my
life.

I trust the process of the universe.

Through darkness, I understand light.

Life is a school for souls. I am where I am
meant to be in my journey.

I allow myself to feel my feelings without
judgment.

I fearlessly face my emotions and move
through them with self-compassion.

I trust the process. I am finding peace with
the ways of the world. I am grateful for
life.

11

THE WHEN

A t first, you may struggle with these affirmations. Your monkey mind is trained to be in a depleted state. Your monkey mind is the ruler of your emotions, and it is always unsatisfied. Just like training muscles, you will train this beast. Like Joe Dispenza's metaphor in his speeches, the monkey mind is like a horse who will get spooked and react to its own detriment. When a mind with higher consciousness gets on the horse, it is now in command, overlooking the vast landscapes of highs and lows. It can see and understand what's going on around it. The horse will eventually be trained to listen to the rider. It will form trust that the rider can see things from above that it does not see. After wrestling with the horse or the monkey mind, you will eventually gain its trust. This is when the monkey mind learns to submit to the greater consciousness.

You can't wait for that healing to feel wholeness. You have to feel wholeness for that healing to occur.

DR. JOE DISPENZA

People use affirmations in different ways. In my experience, what works best is to meditate in the morning and set your intention for the day. At first, my intention would be to compassionately notice my monkey mind throughout the day and bring it back to the big picture with my affirmations. I always associate my affirmations with three deep breaths. Also, in the evening, I will do visualization practices where I vividly picture and put myself into the life of my dreams. I will feel complete fulfillment and gratitude. If you have trouble doing this at first, you can use guided meditations for manifesting your dream life on YouTube. When I take my deep breaths and say my affirmations, I keep this picture and this feeling in my mind and body. It will be uncomfortable at first. You will wrestle with the monkey mind/wild beast. Through consistency, it will get easier and feel more natural.

There has been scientific evidence that listening to affirmations, especially in your own voice, could help you internalize these words. A good practice could be recording affirmations on a platform like "Think Up" and listening to them while you shower or clean. I also recommend writing them down and putting them next to your mirror, in the car or on your desk. Affirmations don't take much time to practice. They are short. The key is to simply create patterns of using them often and keep reminders of them around your day-to-day life. You simply will get results if you practice them regularly.

Remember, it will be hard at first, but stick with it until you normalize it. Think about addictions to toxic partners or alcohol — when you first stop the cycle, it feels very uncomfortable and wrong. After a month of being free of it, you begin to gain a new perspective. After a few months, you may look back and wonder how you ever were in that addictive state to begin with. What you used to be obsessed with simply doesn't hook you anymore.

The most important time to use affirmations, for me, is when I get into a negative self-dialogue. You will go through your day, and then you will notice physical sensations of stress come over you. You will all of a sudden be aware that "I'm doing it." It is an amazing experience to start seeing yourself from the higher consciousness. You will then LOVINGLY notice yourself. You have compassion for you. You remember your process of picking your affirmations based on your wounds. You take three deep breaths to interrupt the chatter. You fill yourself up with that light and higher knowing. You breathe out the black clouds of delusional, self-limiting talk. You reconnect with your affirmations. Why am I here? What is the bigger picture for my life? How can I reconnect with who I truly am and find my inner peace?

I am love. I trust the process. My needs will be met. I am an eternal being. Money flows to me easily. As I take care of those around me, the universe takes care of me. My needs have always been met, and they will continue to do so. I am creating the life of my dreams. I deserve all the abundance this world has to offer. I am grateful.

35 AFFIRMATIONS TO PROMOTE KINDNESS

FREE BONUS MATERIAL

THE
POWER
IN
BEING
KIND

150 SIMPLE ACTS OF KINDNESS

You can't just affirm kindness, you need to
practice kindness! Simple examples you can
EASILY integrate into your life of kindness.

SIGN UP AT:
HTTPS://RACHELRIGGIO.COM

12

CONCLUSION

From ancient practices to neuroscience, we have discovered the true power of affirmations. The law of attraction allows us to believe that we can influence our realities when we know how to utilize our innate power. Co-creation is not something talked about in school, but why not? When we have learned the process and disciplined routine, we can transform the way we think, feel and behave. This recipe has the ability to change our outer environment. We are creating it all.

Unless you've been living a tribal life in nature, you've been programmed to feel inadequacy and self-sabotage. External forces like social media, popular songs and TV shows keep us thinking that we are unworthy. If you really have a heart to heart with yourself, in the silence of all the chatter, I'd say that on a deep level, you know you deserve love and to have your needs met. We may have become accustomed to talking down to ourselves or putting too much pressure on ourselves. The things we are telling ourselves are not necessarily what we believe. It is time to confront that learned behavior and rise above it. It will take awareness and discipline to train the monkey mind, but we have what it takes to move beyond this self-concept. We will change our lives with our decision to become aware of what we are telling ourselves. The things we can imagine for our lives will become a reality as we align our vibration with that of what we desire. Becoming what we desire is attracting what we desire. The law of attraction confirms that like attracts like. How can we vibrate at the frequency of gratitude for things that we want before we receive them in our lives? This is the power of affirmation. It will transform your life. As you normalize your affirmations, you can also repeat and share them with your loved ones. This is one of my favorite quotes:

It is in the sharing of great truths that the consciousness of humanity will attain new heights.

JAIME SAMS

Always come back to gratitude. Stay grateful. If you are grateful, you will attract more to be grateful for. Sharing our experiences and findings on this subject will help us to understand it better. As we make this our reality, we raise our vibration and level of consciousness. Many tribes believe that no one wins until all needs of the tribe are met as a whole. We are all one, and the suffering of others is the suffering of our collective consciousness. Learning this with friends and family can help keep you accountable for your words and actions. Holding ourselves and each other accountable for what we broadcast into the quantum field of creation will be our integrity as we walk the road to inner peace and abundance.

Dare to dream about what your life could be. Let's rise to thrive, together. Please leave us a review, as our intention is to spread this message as far as possible. We believe in a thriving world, where everyone's needs may be met with community, unity and abundance.

ABOUT THE AUTHOR

Life is such a wild ride! I never in 1 million years thought that I'd have my name on the cover of a book! Yet, writing just feels so good and comes so naturally to me! I've been on such a crazy journey from angry addiction in juvenile hall to living in peace with myself in the middle of a rice field running a school. I've been so determined to find peace in my life through all the hardships and I feel so lucky to be able to have the opportunity to write about things that have the potential to higher the vibration of our beautiful world.

Learn More

- Website: https://rachelriggio.com
- Facebook Page: Facebook.com/Rach.Riggio
- FB Group: Facebook.com/LetsRiseToThrive
- Non-Profit: https://theredroadfoundation.org

Other works by the Author:

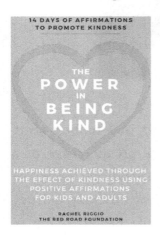

This lovely little book contains -70- beautiful and inspiring affirmations that promote kindness. With a few simple tips on using these affirmations, your journey towards inner peace and happiness will begin.

REFERENCES

Dispenza, 2012, Breaking the Habit of Being Yourself. London: Hay House.

Dyer, W.W. 2012. I am. Hay House.

Tzu, L. (1996). Tae Te Ching (A. Waley, Trans.). Wordsworth Editions.

Alan Watts, 1967. The Book: On the Taboo Against Knowing Who You Are, New York, Collier Books.

Wayne Dyer, 2012. Wishes Fulfilled: Mastering the Art of Manifesting, London, Hay House.

Cohen GL, et al. (2014). The psychology of change: Self-affirmation and social psychological intervention. DOI: 10.1146/annurev-psych-010213-115137.

Voss P, et al. (2017). Dynamic brains and the changing rules of neuroplasticity: Implications for learning and recovery. DOI: 10.3389/fpsyg.2017.01657.

Printed in Great Britain
by Amazon